You're Hired!

An Easy Reference to Impress Interviewers and Get the Job You Deserve

By: Elizabeth Bernard

9781681272603

I0402549

PUBLISHERS NOTES

Disclaimer – Speedy Publishing LLC

Speedy Publishing LLC

40 E Main Street, Newark, Delaware, 19711

Contact Us: 1-888-248-4521

Website: http://www.speedypublishing.co

REPRINTED Paperback Edition: 9781681272603:

Manufactured in the United States of America

DEDICATION

This book is dedicated to Andy. Good luck on your first job!

TABLE OF CONTENTS

Chapter 1- How to Steal a Job from a Prime Candidate

Scoring the interview for the job that you want doesn't have to be rocket science. Sometimes you can score that interview by simply making a phone call. There are many ways that people go about trying to get an interview. The methods of achieving one vary by company. It is best to know what the company's application process is before taking your first step.

Generally, when a company is hiring they post an ad in the newspaper or an online job bank. How to contact them is usually included in the ad as well. You don't want to email a resume to a company that is requesting that you walk in with your resume. You don't want to call a company that requires a faxed resume etc. Ignoring their initial contacting information will guarantee that you will not get that interview because you have already proven that you can't follow simple directions.

Sometimes, you can get a job lead from a friend before the job has been posted. If this is the case, you can either ask the friend to give the employer your resume and cover letter. If your friend doesn't actually work where the lead came from, you can try calling about the position and ask what the application procedure is.

There are four general methods of applying for a job, and they include these basic methods.

Sending a Resume

Some companies prefer that you mail in your resume. For this type of approach, it is best to include a cover letter with your resume. The cover is a basic letter that describes the position that you are interest in and a few details of your qualifications and skills. It is basically your lead in to your resume. Before writing your cover letter, you should know whom the letter is to be addressed to. You never want to begin a cover letter with "Dear Sir or Madame" or "To whom it may Concern". It shows that you have not prepared, and that you are not looking for a specific position with their company, but any job that you can get your hands on. Basically, it is disrespectful to your prospective employer.

Emailing Your Resume

Emailing resumes is becoming a commonplace way for recruiters to get resumes. Most companies offer this method as an alternative to the others. However, there are few tips on how you should go about it.

You should attach your resume as a word document or PDF file. These are the most common formats and what most companies will accept. The subject line should read like this: Smith, John (clerical position). This makes it easy for the recruiter to know who the email is from, and what it pertains to. It also assures that your email will be read.

Sometimes there are specific methods for addressing an emailed resume. Some companies have certain subject line requirements so follow them. If your company wants you to paste your resume, don't send attachments because your email will be deleted right away.

Faxing Your Resume

Again, you will need to include a cover letter when you fax in your resume. If you are not using your own fax machine, be sure to include your proper contact information. The rules for your cover letter are the same as for mailing your resume. More about cover letters will be provided a bit later on in this book.

Walk-In with Your Resume

For this type of application procedure, you will want to dress appropriately. You would want to dress just like you would for an interview. Companies usually ask you to do this if you are going to be working directly with customers. They ask for a walk in because they want to get a look at your grooming habits right away. Sometimes, a walk in will have the employer giving you a brief interview on the spot, to see if they will require a formal interview later. So be on your best and most appropriate behavior.

Also, walk-ins do not require you to bring in a cover letter with your resume. Your appearance is sort of the cover letter. Sometimes, you will be requested to fill out an application form as well. Smile and be polite, no matter who you are talking to. That could be the difference between getting an interview and just taking an extra trip for nothing.

You're Hired!
Telephoning for an Interview

It is not particularly common anymore for companies to ask you to call them for an interview. That is usually saved for jobs that include sales and/or jobs that are not so easily applied for by the other methods. Telephoning for an interview is a bit common when a company requires that you be on the phone a lot. It gives them a feel for the quality and the personality of the person on the phone. When making this type of interview request, always speak in a clean and clear manner. Be polite and prepared to answer any questions that may be asked of you. You might approach the telephone interview like this:

"Hello Mr. Brown, I am Mike Sandal. I am calling with regards to your ad in the Post about the clerical position". If you are asked your experience and/or previous work experience, be prepared to answer quickly and explain how long you have been doing that type of work and give a brief description of your duties.

The correct way to build your resume will be included later on in this manual. It will give you the correct way to format your resume so that it gets noticed for all of the right things.

CHAPTER 2- YOU GOT THE CALL, NOW WHAT?

Once you get the call for the interview, the next thing that you have to do is prepare for it. You can never over prepare for an interview. The more prepared you are, the harder it will be to make mistakes. It is best to prepare yourself emotionally as well as intellectually for an interview. Giving a great interview is not as hard as some may think, but not as easy as others do either. Here are a few things that must be done in order to prepare for your next interview.

You're Hired!

Remember, during an interview, you are a salesman. You are there to sell yourself to your prospective employer. You want to market yourself in the most interesting way possible. Great preparation for the interview is your best bet. A salesman that is knowledgeable, friendly and positive always gets the close.

Do Your Research

It doesn't matter how much knowledge or experience you have about the position that you are trying to get in a company if you don't have a clue that the company is or what they do. It is disastrous to enter into an interview and not be able to tell your interviewer what their company is about. How else are you going to tell them why you feel that you would be a good addition to their company?

A good and less time consuming way to get to know about a company is to look up their website. You can get all of the general knowledge about them that way, including the names of key people and their job titles. (There will be more on that in a minute) You should sift through most of their pages, including the pages that show samples of their work and/or products.

You can also look them up in the media files if there are any. Read the articles about them and soak in as much information as possible. Another thing that would be nice to do is to check out the surrounding area around the company. It makes for a nice breaker during the interview. You can make a comment about a particular monument or resting place nearby.

A trickier way to get a little extra information about the company is to call them on the phone and ask general questions, without referring to yourself as a potential employee. It's a nice way to get the goods on upcoming promotions etc.

Elizabeth Bernard
Know Your Contact

When called for an interview, ask to whom you will be talking to. It is nice to be able to greet your interviewer by name at the beginning of the interview without first being told who they are. It shows that you are on top of things, and have prepared beforehand.

You will also want to do some research on the person that will be conducting your interview. Learn what they do for the company and try to get some samples of their work or achievements in the company.

If you know what department that you are going to work in you may want to get the names of your potential colleagues and superiors prior to the interview as well. This way you can get some information about their roles in the company and the types of work that they have done.

Mention some of the things that you learn about your potential colleagues in the interview and about how much you look forward to working with them in the future. If you can, give an example of their work so that you will appear more sincere.

Practice Your Responses

It is best, if you are prone to nervousness, to practice giving your responses to the questions that may be asked of you. (A list of the most common questions will appear later on in the manual) You should practice your wording and the tone of voice that you plan to use; Try keeping your responses as brief as possible, but with as much detail as you can.

You're Hired!

When you are trying to work out the proper responses to the interviewer's questions, you will also want to practice the art of getting your nerves under control as well as ridding yourself of any other odd habits while talking; like expressing yourself with your hands.

Practice answering your interview questions with a friend. Get his or her opinion about your delivery and gestures. Perhaps your friend will have some nice insights for you to use during the real interview.

Dress the Part

Pre-select your attire the day before your interview. You want to make sure that your clothes do not have any wrinkles or stains on them. Pick an outfit that best suits the type of job that you are applying for. If you are going to work in an office setting, you should dress conservatively. Soft earth tones are best for women. Try to avoid miniskirts and shirts that show too much skin. A nice dark suit is good for a male.

Of course if you are planning to work outdoors or in an artistic environment, you can dress a little more casually. Just be certain to avoid wearing denim jeans, oversized clothing, and under sized clothing. Women should try and avoid wearing too much make-up as well. It gives the wrong impression.

Even in the hotter seasons, you should not wear sandals or gym shoes to an interview. It sends an unprofessional message. The same goes for hats and other accessories.

Get Organized

Make sure that all of the things that you will need for the interview are prepared the day before. Make a checklist of the things that you will need if you have to. You should always have an extra resume handy during the interview. You should also bring with you a note pad to take notes during the interview if needed. (Only write down the important things that you think you will need to remember)If you have a business card, have one handy, it makes for easy contact later, and it also shows that you are professional and may help the employer to remember your name.

CHAPTER 3- THE PROPER INTERVIEW MANNERS

There are many things that you can do that can take some of the pressure off during an interview. The way that you behave is one of the most important. It's not all in the words that come out of your mouth, but often has a lot to do with the mannerisms that you use.

Interviewers are not just wondering if you are skilled enough for the job, they are often wondering if you would fit in nicely with you co-workers. Your personality is a big part of your interview and can make all the difference. Here are some of the little things that you should pay particularly close attention to during an interview.

You do not want to be chewing gum or breathe mints during your interview. You also don't want to speak in slang during your interview either. It is unprofessional and rude.

Show Confidence

You cannot enter into an interview with a defeatist attitude. You cannot mope or exude too much placidity in your manner. It is not inviting, and does not give the impression of a person that you want to face every day.

Be sure of your abilities without appearing cocky or narcissistic. You want to let you interviewer know that you are equipped to perform well at your job, without alienating other workers. You should point out your accomplishments in your field while remaining somewhat humble.

List your accomplishments in a matter of fact way without going into too much detail. I know this sounds repetitive, but you can never get this point too strongly. Understand that body language plays a large part in exuding confidence to others. Sit straight. Practice good posture, and keep your head up.

Keep a Positive Attitude

You should always try to smile and keep a positive outlook during your interview. If what you are hearing something that doesn't sound good to you, don't frown and look disgruntled, just keep a slight smile on your face until it is time for you to say something. Then approach your interviewer with your questions or concerns when the time is appropriate.

Maintain Eye Contact

Keeping eye contact with your interviewer is very important, especially when one of you is speaking to the other. If you are looking around the room or at the items on the interviewer's desk, you will appear uninterested. Just imagine what you would be thinking if you were speaking to him and he was looking all over the room. You would probably think that you already lost the interview.

Body Language

We've touched on this a little bit but you should mind some of the common errors that many people make when they are speaking to others. I've listed some of the common things that you should avoid when sitting through an interview.

- Avoid fidgeting while speaking to your interviewer. It shows a lack of self-confidence.

- Avoid speaking while using overly expressive hand gestures. It is distracting.

- Avoid biting your lips in between sentences. It gives the impression that you are making things up.

- Do not sit with your arms crossed because it makes you appear stand-offish.

- Do not shrug your shoulders when asked a question that you are unsure of. Take a second to think of your response. Shrugging your shoulders gives the impression that you don't know the answer.

- Don't answer with nods and head shakes. Use your words to answer questions.

- Get plenty of sleep the night before the interview. You don't want to yawn in front of the interviewer. He will think that you are expressing boredom.

Your First Impression

First impressions can be a hard thing to get past in any situation. During an interview you want to give the best first impression that you can. There are many small things that you can do to assure that you give the best impression possible. They are as follows:

- You can never be too polite to the person that directs to your waiting area when waiting to be interviewed. A small gesture like, asking how they are doing can work wonders for you when you leave the building later.

- While waiting to be interviewed, sit properly and behave as if everyone passing you by is your potential interviewer. (They just might be) Smile at people as much as possible. Do not act impatient or bored, it sends the wrong message. Some interviewers will keep you waiting just to see how you handle yourself.

- Greet you interviewer with a firm handshake and a smile.

- Remain standing until your interviewer asks you to be seated. It is simply polite and shows proper etiquette.

- Again, dress according to the type of job that you are applying for.

- Show yourself to be well organized, by having all things needed for the interview.

- While waiting do not eat or drink anything.

- Don't chat on your cell phone while waiting for your interviewer. It makes you look distracted.

Your Resume

This may seem like an unimportant thing during an interview, but this is the sole reason why you may get that interview so you should be prepared with a well written resume.

You should tailor your resume to highlight the qualifications, work experience and any education that you've had that best represents the type of work you are applying for. You should also include any other work experience that you've had, as well as any accomplishments that you have made in your field.

You may also want to dress up your resume to let it stand out a bit. A nice border is an elegant way to make your resume stand out without being a distraction to the information within it.

Of course there also quite a few things that recruiters hate to see on resumes as well. Many people do not think that recruiters really go all the way through a resume, but they really do. Recruiters have certain pet peeves when it comes to reading a resume. I've included a list of some of the pet peeves that you should avoid when putting your resume together. These are the things that recruiters hate to see.

- Hiding or not including vital information on a resume is like death. A recruiter needs to see all of your important information without having to search for it.

- Major gaps in your employment history leave a recruiter wondering about your work ethic. Be prepared to answer questions if you have such gaps in yours.

- Summaries that are hard to follow and understand are annoying to recruiters. Keep your summary easy and brief.

- Use easy and simple fonts. Fancy fonts and colors are not eye catching in the manner that you likely wanted it to be. Yours will become to how-to on making resume errors.

- Avoid writing your resume as a narrative or in the first or third person. It is really irritating for a recruiter, and comes off as arrogant and/or egotistical.

- Pictures and/or graphics on a resume are distracting to a recruiter. Things like that will likely get your resume tossed out without a glance.

- Needlessly adding objectives and introductions on your resume bores recruiters. They know what your objective is, and your resume is not meant to be a novel.

- Lying or putting misleading information on your resume is a major no-no. There are always ways for a recruiter to check up on you and many do, so don't lie. Getting caught in a lie on a resume just says that you can't be trusted.

- Adding unnecessary information on a resume like your hobbies is completely useless. You should save that section to describe any accomplishments that you have made in your field.

- Sending a resume that doesn't match the type of job that you are applying for is extremely irritating to a recruiter. You are wasting their time.

- Using overly long paragraphs in a resume will get yours tossed aside. It is harder for the recruiter to read and makes the task take too long.

- Resumes that are more than two pages will not be fully read by a recruiter. That's just the way it is.

- Dating the information in your work history in the wrong order makes your resume harder to follow. (Work history should be listed with most current jobs at the top)

- Resumes that have too much detail when talking about your previous duties are a waste of your time. Duties are generally just sifted through. They are rarely given very much attention, just enough to give the recruiter an idea of what you have done in the past.

- Spelling and grammatical errors just proves that you are not very keen on details.

CHAPTER 4- CRITICAL MISTAKES THAT COULD COST YOU THE JOB

Inadequate Preparation for the Interview

One of the most critical mistakes that you can make in a job interview is to arrive unprepared for the interview. There are too many job seekers out there who do not do any research into the company that they are interviewing for. How can you prove that you are the right candidate for a job or a specific position if you do not know anything about the job for which you are applying?

Benjamin Franklin is known for a famous quote, "By failing to prepare you are preparing to fail.", and this quote is never more applicable than when it comes to preparing for a job interview. It is imperative that you do all of the necessary homework long beforehand. If you come off as an enthusiastic and committed candidate for the job, you will have a much better chance of impressing whoever is interviewing you.

You're Hired!

As soon as you find out that you will be interviewing for a company, research them and the position that you will be interviewing for. This way, you can demonstrate that you are absolutely the right candidate for the job by answering the questions that your interviewer poses effectively and intelligently. You will also be able to prepare the most appropriate questions to ask of your interviewer as well.

The most obvious way to prepare yourself for a job interview is to visit the website for the company that you are interviewing with. You will find a lot of useful information on most company websites. Other website resources that are worth exploring include websites relating to the industry, websites offering business information, and websites belonging to competing companies. You may also want to visit your local library to find out about relevant periodicals and directories.

Another useful idea is to visit the company beforehand, picking up any relevant information and brochures that are available there. You may also feel inclined to observe for a little while. The better prepared that you are for your interview ahead of time, the greater your chances will be for success. You will find that many of the principals in this report tie in together. For example, preparing yourself for your job interview will have a great impact on avoiding a number of the critical mistakes that follow after this one. For example, by researching the employer and company beforehand, you can better prepare yourself both to answer questions posed by the interviewer, and to ask the right questions when prompted.

Preparing yourself with the right information about the company beforehand can have a significant impact on how comfortable and prepared you come across to the employer. This is one of the most ideal ways to prove that you are the right candidate for the job.

Elizabeth Bernard
Arriving Too Early or Too Late

One of the most common mistakes that job seekers make going in to an interview, one that can easily compromise an entire interview is arriving at the wrong time. It is difficult to overcome this initial bad impression created either by arriving too late for the appointment, or by arriving far too early and forcing the interviewer to change their schedule in order to accommodate you.

Luckily, there are a couple of different techniques that you can employ in order to avoid making this seriously costly mistake. It is imperative that you arrive on time to your job interview appointment. You do not necessarily have to arrive at the appointment time on the dot, but a few minutes early are actually preferable. Make sure that you have working directions, which may mean driving them to test the travel time before the actual day of the interview.

You may want to make a complete practice run to make sure that you have the timing right. Make sure that your dry run is completed at the same time as your interview, so you can gauge the traffic at that time during the day. Make sure that you have all of the information that you need long beforehand so that you are not scrambling at the last minute in preparation. For example, you should write down the name of the person that you are supposed to ask for, so that you can go directly to the right place once you arrive.

You should also make sure to bring all of the necessary documentation, which we will touch on later on in this report - But the important consideration to make is that you should gather all of your necessary documentation long beforehand so that you are not scrambling at the last minute to print out resumes, or to gather references and work samples to bring with you.

Arriving in a flustered rush is not a good way to show up to your interview. The whole intention of a job interview is to prove that you are the right candidate for a job, and if you prove your unreliability the first day that you meet the interviewer, you will have difficulty proving otherwise. Being too early for your initial job interview can be just as critical a mistake as arriving late. If you arrive an hour early or more, you may be forcing the interviewer to change their schedule in order to accommodate you, and that is not a good way to get the interview started.

If you want to impress the interviewer by being prompt, aim for 10 to 15 minutes early rather than a whole hour or more. By arriving fifteen minutes early, you have ample time to let the interviewer be notified of your arrival without forcing them to accommodate you long before the interview is set to begin. When it comes to arriving at your job interview, the best thing that you can do is arrive either right on time, or with ten or fifteen minutes to spare.

Arriving late is essentially asking to be dismissed. People who have turned up late for job interviews have literally been turned away, because employers are not looking for people who cannot prove their own selves to be dependable and trustworthy from day one. Your interview is your first impression to your prospective employer, and your main intention should be to impress future employers in as many ways as you can.

Having the Wrong Attitude

There are a number of different behaviors during an interview that can cause you to come across as a negative person, or simply a person who does not have the right positive attitude for the job in question. Coming across as a negative person can be the result of a wide variety of different behaviors that occur during the interviewing process. For example, if you should happen to make

Elizabeth Bernard

complaint regarding previous jobs, positions, bosses, coworkers, colleagues or companies can send a rather negative message to your prospective employer, and should be avoided at all costs. Something else that can create a negative impression is inappropriate body language.

The following body language actions can all offer a negative message to the person who is interviewing you

- Hunching down

- Slumping in the chair

- Avoiding eye contact with the interviewer

- Looking down constantly

- Folding your arms over your chest

- Fiddling with your hair

- Fiddling with items on the desk

There are also a number of verbal and non-verbal signals that give off a negative attitude to the person who is interviewing you, including but not limited to

- speaking inaudibly

- speaking quietly

- mumbling

- The use of words like 'like' or 'um' repeatedly

You're Hired!
It is important that you practice your answers to test interview questions, and your questions about the company in front of a mirror in order to improve the tone of your voice and your positive body language. By practicing beforehand, you can eliminate flaws in your interview demeanor which can give you a better chance of being successful in your interview.

Being Unprepared for Interview Questions

There are two important elements to a job interview.

The first is the questions that the interviewer asks of you, and the second is the questions that you ask of the interviewer in return. If you are unable to properly articulate the right answers to the interview questions that are asked of you, you will most certainly have difficulty conveying the fact that you are the ideal candidate for the position to the person who is interviewing you.

The best way for you to avoid this practice is to think about your answers and to prepare them beforehand. There are many resources for common job interview questions, and most employers within different industries ask the same questions or at least similar sets of relevant questions which means that you can be prepared to a certain degree no matter what job you are applying for.

Prepare your answers to the most common job interview questions within your industry long before your interview. What questions is most likely going to be asked during the interview? What is normally required of a successful candidate for the position that you are applying for? There are a number of basic or general questions that tend to crop up in almost all job interviews, including but not limited to the following questions

- What are your strengths, or what is your greatest strength?

- What are your weaknesses, or what is your greatest weakness?

- Why do you want this job position?

- What are some of your achievements to date? What has been your greatest achievement in your working history?

- Why are you the ideal candidate for this position? Why should we employ you rather than another candidate?

- If we were to call up your former employer or employers, what would they say about you?

Prepare and practice the answers to questions like these, and you will be able to avoid this critical initial job interview mistake. You do not want to suddenly go blank during the interview process, and this can easily be avoided simply by preparing beforehand and figuring out the most effective answers in order to appear both confidant and poised to the employer who is interviewing you.

Not Asking the Right Questions

There are two important elements to a job interview.

The first is the questions that the interviewer asks of you, and the second is the questions that you ask of the interviewer in return. At some point during the job interview, the person interviewing you is going to ask "Do you have any questions for me?" And this is a question that makes a lot of people tremble. Failing to ask the right, most appropriate questions simply shows a lack of interest and forethought. As a result, this is one of the most critical mistakes that a job interview candidate can make.

You're Hired!

Use the company research that you conducted earlier based on Critical Job Interview Mistake number 01, and prepare questions about the company that are insightful as the best and most efficient way to impress the interviewer you are working with. This will also help you gain the information that you need in order to make the most well informed job decision possible.

During your job interview, you should not sit like a bump on a log. Instead, you should make a real effort to show interest in the company, which can easily be done by asking the employer excellent interview questions in return. This shows the interviewer that you are interested in the company and that you have done your research and arrived prepared. Here are some of the questions that you may want to ask your interviewer. Keep in mind that when asked"

Do you have any questions for me?", "Hmm, nope" is NOT a good answer.

• What are your biggest challenges?

• What is the average day like for this particular position?

• What specific tasks will be expected of me in this position?

• What is the next step following the interview?

• Is this a newly created job position or am I replacing another employee?

• How will my job performance be measured?

• What are the immediate goals of the department that I will be working in?

- What is the biggest challenge that the company is currently facing?

- What competitive advantages does the company have over other similar companies?

- What does the interviewer like best about the company?

- What could I do within this role that would make your job (The employer's job) easier?

- Is there anything else that I can further clarify for you?

- How do I compare with other candidates that have already been interviewed?

Dressing Inappropriately

Another critical mistake that many people make when it comes to initial job interviews should not come as a surprise: Dressing inappropriately. While most people seeking jobs know that dressing appropriately is a big part of arriving prepared to a job interview, most people do not actually have a good understanding of what "dressing appropriately" actually means. As a result, many people arrive at their interview dressed inappropriately, either in general or based on the dress code in question.

As it was mentioned before, it is important to research the company that you are interviewing with beforehand. This comes in handy for a number of different reasons, one of which is so that you can dress according to the dress code that the rest of the employees are abiding by. By visiting the company before hand and doing a little bit of observing, you can figure out what style of dress would be ideal.

You're Hired!

Get to know the culture of the company. If the company's employees are all wearing conservative clothing, then business casual is not going to cut it when you arrive at your interview. If you want to look like you already belong with the company, which should be your aim to begin with, then it is important that you dress not only to impress, but also to fit in at the same time. You also need to avoid appearances that are excessive, extreme, bright or loud

Resist the temptation to wear colors that are bright, perfumes or body mists that are strong in smell, loud nail polish, or extravagant jewelry. If you have tattoos, cover them up. If you have piercings that are inappropriate, such as earrings for men, or anything other than earrings for women, take the jewelry out or cover the piercings with a band aid. It is important that your interviewer focuses on your skills, your accomplishments and the real reasons for why you are the best candidate for the job, rather than your appearance.

If your appearance fits in with the dress and appearance of the other employees in the company, your interviewer will be able to focus on your strengths rather than your loud appearance or the fact that your dress does not fit in with the company.

Asking about Salary or Benefits

While we have already touched on asking the right questions, we did not really focus on refraining from asking the WRONG ones. One of the biggest initial job interview mistakes that you can make is to ask about salary or benefits during your interview.

The appropriate time for you to discuss compensation and benefit information is once a real, firm offer has been placed on the table. You should refrain from bringing this topic up prematurely. Take the time to learn more about the company and the position that the company is looking to fill. In the end, money is not everything, and is definitely not what you should be obsessing about before you have even fully proven yourself to the company that you are interviewing with.

Career satisfaction comes in a variety of different forms, so focus on joining a collaborative team environment with plenty of opportunity for growth rather than worrying about the benefits package. During the interview process, you should focus and concentrate on the things that really matter - Not compensation.

There are a number of other questions that should be avoided during the initial job interviewing process. The following is a list of questions in addition to "What is my salary?" that you should avoid at all costs when interviewing with a potential employer.

• How long does it take to be promoted?

While it may be fruitful to ask about advancement within the company, it is more important that you focus on the job that you are actually interviewing for.

• When will I be able to take a vacation?

If you are already asking this question at the interview, then you are already thinking about taking time off, and this does not look good to the employer.

• Will I be required to work overtime?

Asking about the hours that you will work says that you are the type of person who likes to watch the clock, and this is not something that a hiring manager is going to want to look for.

• What kinds of employee activities are held?

This question can be a real interview killer. It tells the interviewer that you are more interested in the company activities than in working hard and moving up within the company. Wait until you are hired before you begin to ask questions like this.

• What can I use my company computer for?

Even though many employees use their computers for purposes other than for company work, you should never bring this up during an interview. This shows both a lack of maturity and a lack of business sense as well.

• Will I be able to work from home?

While this may appear to be a good question, new employees need to come to understand the dynamics and the politics of the office before they should even begin to think about working at home. New employees cannot learn anything about the tempo, the faces, the politics and the dynamics of the company if they are working at home.

The hiring manager is going to be looking for someone who will be right there all the time, both working and soaking up the dynamics of the office in order to become more successful and to make the company more successful as well.

While many of these questions may seem naïve, and when you see them in print you may wonder why anyone would ever think to ask them, all of these questions have been asked through numerous job interviews in the past. So there are people out there who are naïve enough to ask these questions in job interviews

And many of them do not understand why they did not land the job after the fact. Not only is it important to know what questions not to ask, it is also important to have a small list of questions that you SHOULD ask, so that you can be prepared when the person interviewing you asks "Is there anything that you want to ask me?" The only thing worse than asking an interview killer of a question, is simply saying "No".

Not Arriving with the Right Documents

Just because you were called in for an interview, it simply does not mean that your prospective employer has a copy of your resume or curriculum vitae on hand. Many employers conduct group interviews, so they may not necessarily be prepared to work with you by keeping your documents handy. It would be a large and critical mistake for you to arrive to your job interview without the documents that you need. Make sure that you bring several copies of your resume so that everyone who attends the interview can have a copy and so that copies can be passed around as needed. Not only will this help you prepare yourself and your interviewers for the interview, but it will also show the person or people interviewing you that you had the consideration and foresight to come into the interview room prepared.

Make sure that you have a portfolio put together if your job interview requires it. Make sure that you have copies of any and all necessary documentation, including your resume, your curriculum vitae, recommendations, references, work samples, and anything else that is required in order to prove your work as a candidate for the job that you are applying for.

Before your interview, it is important that you have the right documents prepared. This should include directions to the interview site, and you should make sure you have enough time not only to get there, but also to find a parking space depending on the driving directions. Make sure that you are leaving early so that you can arrive between ten and fifteen minutes.

Make sure that you have extra copies of your resume, along with a list of references both personal and professional, a notepad so that you can take notes, a daily planner, and a pen and a pencil so that you can take notes and make other important notations during your interview. You may be able to enhance your professional look by carrying a portfolio, a folder or a briefcase. You should also make sure to know the details, such as the name and the title of the person you are supposed to meet with. You should also have conducted research on the company that you are applying for. If you have taken notes on the research of the company, you may want to bring them and continue adding to them as you interview, but only as long as you are willing to let the interviewer see what notes you have already taken.

This is a testament to what information you find most important in your job search. Prepare for the toughest questions so that you will not have to pause when asked important things, such as "Where do you see yourself in 5 to 10 years?" Having the right paperwork and documents prepared is the best way to arrive at an interview. Arriving on time, with your resume or curriculum vitae in hand, and work samples or other information as needed is a great way to show your prospective employer not only that you are taking this job interview seriously, but also that you are hardworking and dependable, and that you know how to make a good impression on the people who really matter within the company. The more prepared you are, the more successful you will be.

Elizabeth Bernard
Being Dishonest or Impolite

Your overall attitude has a lot to do with how your prospective employers perceive you and your candidacy for the position they are hiring for. There are a couple of things that you can do to make sure that your prospective employer or interview you sees you in the right light and does not get the wrong idea. Here are two things that you absolutely need to keep in mind

Dishonesty

You should never, ever lie to an employer under any circumstances to get the position that you want. By lying or being dishonest in general, you are greatly undermining your own abilities and strengths, and you are destroying any trust or rapport that has been developed by the interviewer. If you are unable to get the position that you want based on your current skills or potential skills and accomplishments, then you probably should not be applying for that particular position anyway.

Applying for a position that is beyond your capabilities is simply asking for trouble. Being dishonest about your capabilities to get a job that is beyond your means is an even greater and more dangerous risk. Being Impolite - you need to keep in mind that the person who is interviewing you may very well be your future boss or employer. You should not sit down until you are asked to.

If you want to take off your jacket, you should ask for permission first. If refreshments are offered, thank your host. You should make a point to express your interest toward the job or position that you are interested in applying for and you should also make a point to thank the person interviewing you for the time that they took to sit and speak with you. Even if you are no longer interested in the job that you are applying for by the end of your interview, the person who you sat down and spoke with may still be an excellent contact person with you. You should absolutely never ever burn any bridges with potential employers or other people working within your industry of choice because there is no telling whether or not they will be helpful for you in the future.

If you managed to obtain a job interview through an agency, you should also give them a phone call promptly following your interview so that you can advise them of whether or not you are interested in the role that you are interviewing for.

A large part of your interview success will hinge on your attitude, your willingness to listen, your willingness to ask and answer questions, and your ability to be honest and to have a positive outlook on the interview situation. If you are not projecting the right attitude and appearance to your prospective employer, you will have great difficulty when it comes to proving that you are the right candidate for the job, especially when there is a lot of competition for the job in question.

Marketing Yourself Incorrectly

This is another vital and critical mistake that needs to be avoided in your initial job interview. It is imperative that you market yourself correctly in your job interview in order to be successful when proving yourself as the ideal candidate for a specific company or position. You need to be able to define yourself properly, and to map out your skills to the skills that the job you are applying for requires. You need to know what your major strengths are, and your major accomplishes, especially as they relate to the job that you are hoping to apply and interview for.

You need to use the questions you ask and the answers to the questions the interviewer asks to make you really stand out. Your goal should be to become memorable in the eyes of your future employer without standing out in a negative way. If you have unusual job experiences, interesting skills, unusual hobbies or other characteristics that will help you stand out from the other candidates applying for the job, and then you should bring this up in a way that is natural.

Now should not be the time to name drop, and you should not be aiming to make the interviewer feel uncomfortable or inadequate in any way.

CHAPTER 5- APPLYING FOR YOUR FIRST JOB

- Tell me what your most rewarding college experience was.

- What extracurricular activities did you participate in?

- What have you learned in college that applies directly to this job?

- How have you prepared yourself for the transition from college to the workplace?

- Are you going to graduate school? If so, do you plan to continue working as well?

- How do you plan to manage graduate school and working?

- Did you get any hands on experience in College?

- How do you feel that college has prepared you for this job?

- Have you ever done an internship that helped to prepare you for this type of work?

- What do you think is the best asset that you could bring to the company?

Questions That You Should Ask Your Interviewer

Just like you will be fielding questions from your interviewer, it is best to ask a few of your own. It shows that you are genuinely interested in working there, and that you have some concerns of your own. It also shows that you feel relatively certain that this is the place for you.

Asking the right questions to your prospective employer will show him/her that you are serious in you efforts to work for their company, and that you are an organized individual. You should steer clear of asking any personal questions or any questions that are not directly job related.

If you wish, you may jot down some of the answers that you are given for reference later on. Keep your questions simple and polite. Make sure that you are asking direct questions about the job and/or work environment.

Here are some questions that you should ask your prospective employer:

- Why is this position available right now?

- How many times has this position been filled in the past 5 years?

- What should the new person do that is different from the last person that had this position?

- What would you most like to see done in the next 6 months?

- What are the most difficult problems that this job entails?

- How much freedom do I have in the decision making process?

- What are my options for advancement?

- How has this company succeeded in the past?

- What changes do you envision in near future for this company?

- What do you think constitutes success in this job?

Questions Employers Cannot Ask

Just like there are many questions that an interviewer can ask, there are many that he cannot ask. Some questions are illegal to ask. Many people don't realize that there are off limit questions for employers. That is why I felt that it was important to include them.

When or if you do encounter some of these questions there are ways that you can choose to respond to them. Since some people would probably answer them, it is good to know that you don't have to answer those kinds of questions. You can simply ask how those questions pertain to the job you're applying for. Here is a list of the questions that are illegal for an interviewer to ask.

- Questions about your age are not allowed during an interview because it should not be a factor upon hiring you.

- Questions about your marital status are inappropriate and can easily be mistaken for sexual harassment. This question also applies to whether or not you have children, your child care plans etc. This type of question also includes any other aspect of your personal life that should not affect your chances of being hired.

- Questions about your personal health are also off limits.

- Questions about your ethnicity should not be asked by an interviewer or answered by the person being given the interview.

- Your sexual preference cannot be a factor in your chances of being hired either. This type of question should not be asked.

- Whether or not you have disabilities is a question that should not be asked either.

- Your arrest record is information that doesn't have to be answered. All an interviewer can ask you is if you have ever been convicted of a crime, they cannot ask you what for or how many times.

- Basically, personal information cannot be asked by an interviewer. It is illegal, and you do not have to respond.

The Post Interview Follow-up

Now that the interview is over, the hard work is over, but you still have to follow up on the interview later. Sending a thank you note is the best way to start. The thank you letter should be written with your thanks for their time and consideration in seeing you.

You're Hired!

If you haven't heard from the employer within a week, you should call the office to ask if they have reached a decision yet. This is not being pushy; it shows your enthusiasm and persistence. If they haven't reached a decision, ask when you might expect to hear from them. If they don't give an answer try again in another week and so on.

What Employers Are Looking For

When an employer decides to conduct an interview with you, there are certain things that they are looking for from you. Naturally, you are likely to focus on these things during an interview, but you should remember all of the tips in this manual because following those tips is what is going to make the employers see all of those things in you.

Since everybody wants to have a leg up when it comes to an interview, it naturally seemed to be appropriate to let you in on what the employers are evaluating you on during an interview. So here is that list.

• Your Enthusiasm: Employers want to know that you are willing and eager to be a part of their company. Being fully stocked with knowledge about the company is a sure fire way to show your enthusiasm.

• Your ability to speak clearly: If you approach an interview mumbling and speaking slang, a prospective employer will not see you as a professional.

• Showing your teamwork skills: You should show an example of your ability to work as a team during your interview.

- Leadership skills: You should show your leadership abilities by approaching your interview with an offensive train of thought.

- Problem solving ability: Employers needs to know that you can handle yourself when a problem arrives.

- Work related experience: You definitely want to show that you have some experience in the field already, so that the employer knows that you will not be overwhelmed.

- Community involvement: Employers love to see that you have done volunteer work. It shows that you take pride in your community, and a willingness to be a team player.

- Company knowledge: Again, this stipulates that employers like to see that you have done your research about their company. It shows that your interest in working for them is sincere.

- Flexibility: Employers want to know that you are able to go with the flow. It proves that they can depend on you later.

- Ambition and Motivation: Ambitious people are generally motivated enough to make great improvements in the company as they are working their way up the ladder. Ambition usually means more money for the company.

- People skills: Your ability to get along with others is very important to an employer. They need to know that you won't ruffle any feathers when you are hired.

- Professional appearance: Nobody wants a slob working in their office. Be certain to dress appropriately for the job that you are applying for.

- Ability to Multitask: This is getting to be a very necessary skill in the workplace. Most days, you will be required to multitask. Even if you are not, employers need to know that you can do it without freaking out on them.

- Computer ease: These days, just about every company in the world is running on computers. The ability to work a computer with at least minimal amount of ease is important. It is best to keep a leg up on the most common software like MS Office, Quark Express, and Linux.

- Reliability: Employers want dependable and reliable people to work for them. Your ability to arrive on time is a good place to start when trying to prove that you possess this quality.

Employer Evaluations

Employers are generally monitoring and evaluating you on three skill sets during an interview. Those three skill sets can easily be broken down into these sections:

Content Skills

These are the skills that are directly related to performing a specific job in your profession. You get these skills by learning your craft in an accredited school through specialized training, work experience, attaining a degree, and internships. This shows an employer that you are have acquired all of the knowledge that you will need to perform your job efficiently.

If you do not have this type of skill available, you can simply express that you are looking into specialized training, and/or would be willing to start. It may not be exactly what the employer is looking for, but it shows that you show initiative.

Functional Skills

These are the skills that reflect your ability to work with others, and how you incorporate data. This is where an employer decides whether or not you are a team player. You can display this skill by displaying your past employment record and accomplishments that are directly job related.

Generally an employer will get an idea of your ability to work with others depending on your reasons for leaving previous jobs, whether or not you were fired before etc. If you have been fired before, don't lie about it, and do not act bitter about it when discussing the reason, this will not benefit you in the end. Be forthcoming and sincere. Express that it was a learning experience for you and tell them what you learned from it. It reflects well on your temperament.

Adaptive Skills

This is a general show of your personality and temperament. It also covers yourself management skills. During your interview, the employer will be evaluating you on your general ability to get along with him/her. Your general personality traits are monitored during this time.

When faced with a difficult question, you do not want to get defensive or angry. Just take a few seconds to think about what you should say rather than say something you will regret. If you must; simply explain that you are a little nervous so that you can buy a few extra seconds to answer.

You want to appear at ease, (or as much so as you can) during your interview. You want the employer to think that you anticipated

You're Hired!

everything that he/she is going to say. Even if you are terrified at your replies, do not let them see you sweat.

ABOUT THE AUTHOR

Elizabeth Bernard is a career counselor at the University of Arizona. For over 30 years, she has helped thousands of students get started on a career.

Elizabeth was born in the UK in 1962. When she was five years old, her family moved to the US in search of a greener pasture. A bright child, Elizabeth learned quickly and graduated at the top of her class. She got in the University of Arizona and was awarded a full scholarship.

Now a mother, Elizabeth continues to give valuable pieces of advice to fresh graduates and young professionals.